"Listen, You Can Make It Through This."

~God

Mevely Spell

The You Can, You Will Motivator

"Listen, You Can Make It Through This."

~God

Copyright © 2022 by Mevely Spell

ISBN (979-8-9862446-0-0)

Disclaimer: The following versions of the Bible may have been referenced: New International Version (NIV), King James Version (KJV), New Living Translation (NLT), English Standard Version (ESV), New King James (NKJV), New International Reader's Version (NIRV), Christian Standard Bible (CSB), Common English Bible (CEB), The Message (MSG).

MTE Publishing
mtepublishing.com

Acknowledgements & Dedication

I would like to thank my Creator, the one who carefully and purposely knitted me in my mother's womb and allowed me to finish my story and share it with the world. Saying thank you will never be enough because I owe You, my life. Therefore, I am committed to serving You, Lord, for the rest of my life! At 20-something, You promised me that I would make it through, and You kept your word. So, God it is You [and you alone] whom I faithfully depend upon for protection, provision, and every heart's desire.

I dedicate this literary work to my children: Shalonda, Devonia, and Darneshia. You're my reasons to keep going. You ladies are the healed version of myself. Walk in wholeness and holiness. I also dedicate this work to my grandchildren. You all are my other reasons to keep fighting the good fight of faith. I am proof that you, too, can make it through.

Additionally, I would like to acknowledge four individuals: My uncle, the late Rev. Dr. George E. McRae, Sr., Supt. Herbert Colbert, Pastor Jarvis F. Wright, Sr., and Rev. James "Jimmy" Sloan. You all have played a vital role in my Christian walk. Each of you taught me the word of God and allowed me to serve you [and the people of God] with grace, passion, humility and commitment. I appreciate your leadership and accountability as respected mentors, brothers, and friends in Christ, I have called on you (and your wives) to help me make it through and I am still here because of God and your prayers.

Listen, I am finally at peace with my past, present, and future...and with God's grace, I will continue to make it through, He promised.

Table of Contents

Foreword
Two Decades of Realness and a Lifetime of Faith

God has brought me through different situations (Isaiah 43:1-2).

I came to know Mevely Spell through church, and we became better acquainted when we served on the same evangelistic outreach team. Evangelist Spell is authentic, and she genuinely loves people. Her realness is the gravitational pull that attracts strangers to her (and vice versa). Evangelist Spell is a Godsend... for anyone who has had the opportunity to experience her.

There are some people who don't believe in a real God. Nevertheless, our experiences and faith give us the audacity to keep going and believe. Not in spite of anything, but because we made it through what could have killed us! This is faith and God at work. Evangelist Spell's life proves that God truly uses every aspect of our lives to ensure that those who love God, and who are righteous, are *never* forsaken.

To those who have decided to read this literary work, the peace and freedom you'll experience will transform your faith. Sometimes, life's struggles have the propensity to put us in a self-imposed prison. However, Evangelist Spell's life proves that nothing is more freeing and real than God's faithfulness and love towards us. It's the way in which these things beautifully manifest that helps us to understand that when we *listen* to God and trust His word we can make it though *anything*!

Grace, Mercy, and Love,

Dr. Argatha Gilmore

Dear BFF

We're finally here! Faithfully, we knew this day would come. Undoubtedly, the assignment on your life was established in your mother's womb. God had to make good on His promises – you've endured more pain and hardship than most people I know.

From the first day we met, I knew there was something divinely special about you. I have witnessed your brokenness and your breakthroughs! Surprisingly, through it all, you still showed up as a dedicated sister, loving wife, and an amazing mother. Most importantly, I watched, firsthand, your supernatural transformation.

You've weathered life's storms without trying to evacuate–you bent your knees and escaped to God's presence. You held your head up high, kept your faith intact, and put on the full armor of God. Not to mention, you followed the play book of life [the Bible] with prayer and fasting, you made it through – test after test and trial after trial!

Even when you waivered, you still held fast! I knew your life and purpose could not be in vain. God had to come through, especially for you! Your cries will touch the souls of so many women [and men]. You are an AMAZING person and woman of God, and I am elated about your journey ahead. Continue to be a beacon of light and hope to the world as you help others know that "they, too, can make it through!"

Love,

Cindy

Introduction
Trauma from the Start

My stepdad murdered my mom, and as unfortunate as it sounds that wasn't the beginning because I was born into trauma. However, my traumatic childhood trained me to never retreat. Therefore, I mastered how to weather every storm until it passed. This is how I learned to make it through. Trauma equipped me to stand, pray, and believe that I could and would make it through anything. It was through a series of crises and chaos that led me on a journey of knowing God, personally.

Leading up to the horrific murder suicide in 1984, there was always fussing, cussing, fighting, and drinking between my mom and stepdad [I called him dad].

It happened on a Tuesday. My fiancé and I had been together the Sunday before, and my parents had just left. Now we didn't have the best relationship, but we had one. I told my fiancé that dad was going to kill mom and then kill himself. Words have power even when the reality of what we're facing is unbearable.

At the time, my dad was an alcoholic. He was going to doctor appointments to help manage his addiction. That particular Tuesday, I was supposed to take him to his appointment. I didn't really know the voice of God back then, but something said take him when you get off work. I had no clue that was the day he'd kill my mom and himself.

While at work, at the grocery store, I looked out the window and saw them pass by and I thought to myself, "where are they going?" Then my fiancé came by and told me not to leave work until he came back. Minutes later, my aunt's sister came to the store. She told my manager, I needed to go home. I got in her car and asked, "Is something going on with dad?" She shook her head and didn't say another word.

When I arrived at the house, there appeared to be a million police officers everywhere. As I made my way through the crowd, I asked my uncle where mom was because I needed to take care of her. The look in his eyes said, "she's gone". My brother Freddie was the one who found them dead in the house. The Sunday before, he and my mom had an argument. He went to their house to make peace about the situation but discovered it was too late.

After mom died, I remember going through a lot of different emotions and asking lots of questions. Then finally, I got peace when I heard a voice say, "You're going to be OK, and you *can* make it through this."

I was 20-years-old and that's when I knew that if I survived the tragic death of my mother, I would make it through anything. I needed those encouraging words in so many seasons throughout life.

My life began to spiral, and things got worse from there. Nevertheless, I knew God was going to bring me through. This was my blessed assurance. I had to accept going through my whole adult life without parents. I never knew my birth father (my real dad) and my mom was viciously murdered, but God has been with me. Sometimes I sit back and think, God really brought me through all of these things and warm tears of gratitude [not sadness] flow down my cheeks. So, with a grateful and courageous heart, I can boldly declare the words, "Listen, you can make it through this." ~God

Chapter 1

Who's My Daddy

The same man that violently murdered my momma also molested me as a child. This was just the beginning of my personal testimony.

My mom never told me who my real father was. I was hopeful the day she took me to the Putnam County Health Department that I would find out my father's identity. I was 15-years-old and pregnant. The triage nurse came into the room to collect information. When she asked about my mom, she said her name and when she was supposed to give my dad's name, she said, "it didn't matter", but to me it did. I desperately wanted and needed to know. I needed that missing piece to my life's puzzle.

Although my stepfather adopted me, he was still a ruthless man. The people in our community believed he was a "good" person; however, they didn't know him when he was drunk. He worked 3 p.m. -11 p.m., Monday through Friday and would drink from the time he got off until Sunday night [just in time to sober up for work on Monday]. Colt 45 turned him into a monster.

However, I have to give him credit for my independence because he would get drunk and say spiteful things followed by demeaning actions. I remember when he would throw his checkbook down the hallway and say, "Tell your daddy to pay for your lunch this week." The absence of my biological father was the biggest void in my life well into my adulthood. Not a day went by that I didn't wonder who my father was. I'd look at strange men and ask myself, "Could he be my father?"

I knew the area where my dad was from. My brother also was familiar with the vicinity and before he died, he told me to go to Clearwater, FL. and search for my dad. I wondered for years who I really was. Then one day, it's like the Lord took that away from me. It was like, God said, "It doesn't matter who your father is, I am your father now." Something clicked and at that moment my birth father's identity didn't matter anymore. I didn't question it anymore and God made me whole. My biological dad fathered me and that was his sole purpose.

My daughters still want me to search for him, but my attitude is different now. Whoever my father is, it is his loss, not mine. Although it was hard growing up without my real daddy, my spiritual father is the best thing that ever happened to me.— God.

Chapter 2

His Nasty Hands

The sexual abuse started when I was around 10-years-old...The age most little girls are still playing with dolls and exploring the world around them. The molestation lasted for a long period of time.

My mom didn't work much. She cut cabbage and did odd jobs here and there. When she had a job *that* was the pastime of the day [him fondling me]. Back then, schools were on block schedules. So, when I had afternoon classes, I was home with him during the morning and that's when he'd molest me. The abuse happened almost daily during my middle school years. I had to dodge him to keep him from feeling on me. I was maturing and starting to develop. Then he would offer me money that I didn't want in exchange for sex. I wanted him to leave me alone but there seemed to be no end in sight [or at least I thought]. That period of my life was a really bad time, but I always knew trouble wouldn't last. Sleepovers were common for teenage girls, but I never wanted my friends to stay over [although they did from-time-to-time] because I feared him getting his hands on them. When they stayed the night, I used my dresser or bed as a barricade to keep them safe. This put my mind at ease. I just didn't want any of my friends to experience my despair.

The abuse went on until I started my menstrual cycle, and he was the first to know. Everything I did or went through, he was there. I got pregnant at 15. I remember praying as an adolescent: God send somebody...anybody to save me! Then God gave me my first born, Shalonda, she saved my life.

This is why I don't judge teen moms because not all of them are "being fass." I was called "fass" but I wasn't. Listen! I am a survivor of a horrible situation and I made it through!

People don't understand the relationship I have with my "baby daddy" who eventually became my husband. Although the pregnancy was unplanned, it was a blessing. My pregnancy stopped the sexual abuse, which by that time was full-blown sex with my stepdad. The unplanned pregnancy gave me a way out. I didn't know it then, but the word of God declares that He wouldn't put more on us than we can bear, and I was at my breaking point.

My boyfriend became my savior at that period in my life. At that time, I wondered why he even talked to me. I had low self-esteem and Lord knows I didn't feel pretty. Even after the Lord saved me, I never felt I could be enough [until a couple of years ago]. Listen, God delivered me from that, *too*! Nevertheless, growing up, people thought our family had it all together but at the same time, it was a house of horrors.

One day my brother came across the family pictures from various trips we took and the photos with me standing next to my stepdad were always torn off. I thought it was weird. My brother looked at me and said, "That explains it." I knew what he was talking about. This man was in love with me, and I deeply despised him for what he did to me for so many years; however, I could never bring myself to hate him.

Chapter 3

I Just Wanted My Momma
to Love Me

When I was around 13-years-old, momma caught him in the act. Finally, she was going to save me, [or so I thought]! I was on my knees fondling him with my hands and he was sitting in a squeaky rocking chair. For years I couldn't stand that sound. My mom called him a bastard and grabbed me by the hand, and we walked to the convenience store. Momma bought me ice cream.

She never asked any questions. However, from that point on, I became the problem. My mother's love dwindled away and her hatred towards me [seemingly] increased. Her words hurt! "You're a whore and a slut! Why can't you be like all the other little girls…

like the girl next door?" I was everything but a child of God! She said, "You need to be more respectable". And to think, I was the one who was disrespected and violated, daily. I loved my mom [most girls really do]. It's how God intended it to be. However, my abuse was somehow my fault. I never hated my mom, I just hated what she allowed to happen, and even now, I realize she wasn't equipped to help me. I later learned my mom suffered from mental illness and spent time in a state mental hospital. She was raised by my uncle. While I don't know what her trauma was, surely, she could not save me [that was God's job]. So, my momma could only meet our basic needs [food, clothing, shelter] - nothing more, and a whole lot less.

Nevertheless, my mom and dad would fight for blood. One time there was a really bad fight, and my dad folded my brother up into a mattress. His arms and legs went through the box springs; I just wanted to protect him and that's what I did. Whenever I jumped in to stop the fights my dad would stop, but that meant that he would come into my room later that night and have his way with me.

My mom was a big woman and definitely a bad woman, too. She would get the ax and go after my dad. We lived in a nice four bedroom, two bath home. Mom would chop the door off and get back into the house following a fight. She would also break out windows [in doors and cars] -- she never seemed afraid.

Often, she escaped the scene battered and bloody with me and my brother. We often left in the wee hours of the morning and walked to a family friend's house [we considered our grandma]. To this day, I still don't understand how anyone can stay with a man who molest their children. Then again, my mom was trapped, she didn't have an education, nothing to aspire to in life and nowhere to go. So, she did what she had to do to provide the basic necessities for her children. Listen, I'm not here to judge anyone, I only want to help. And when you put your mind to it, add prayer; it will happen for you!

Chapter 4

Motherhood Came Naturally

I had Shalonda [my first baby] in 1979 and a year later, I knew I had to leave Palatka. This was during my senior year; I had to get away from the dysfunction. So, I moved to Daytona with my boyfriend's sister who was attending Bethune Cookman University. She'd sneak me into her dorm so I would have somewhere to stay. Eventually, she found an apartment for us. I didn't have a job or a car [I didn't even have a driver's license]. I had to walk miles to find a job, but I was determined not to be a statistic. I didn't want to be on welfare and unable to take care of my baby. In the back of my mind, thoughts of not making it through, haunted me. So, I left her behind with her dad and he'd bring her for visits. She was growing up so fast and so was I. It was one good sacrifice that was well worth it. I had to make a better life for me and my daughter.

I remember looking everywhere for a job. While in high school, one day I was in the lunch line, and I overheard someone say something about a girl named Jewel. Then I refocused my hearing and I heard, "Jewel T is hiring" [that's what God wanted me to hear]. When school ended, I went straight to Jewel T and I asked if I could fill out an application and the man said "yes". He called me back for a job interview and I got the job. I prayed and I knew God gave me that job. I have had many tests and trials on this job! I have been at the same job for 40 years now. That's why I'm so grateful because this is the job that provided for my family, kept my children from going to jail and it kept them off the streets. It kept a roof over our heads and food to eat. When I first started, I was working 20-30 hours, but God. He is the perfect provider!

During my 12th- grade year, I made the A-B honor roll [while I was working], this was the only time I ever received academic recognition. Thankfully, in 1981, I graduated from Spruce Creek High School in Volusia County. I felt so accomplished, and I knew undoubtedly that God had brought me through! I cried joyfully. My parents sat in the crowd proudly and admired me, their daughter, a teenage mom who was said to be nothing more than a slut. But God said otherwise... and I listened! I beat the odds. When God is for us, the odds are always in our favor.

Chapter 5

Cheating was Okay… Molestation I Ain't Play

After graduation, I returned to Palatka and eventually married the man who saved what was left of me. We got married in 1987. We left his grandaddy's funeral and got married at his uncle's house in Crescent City. Rev. Sloan married us, he also led me to Christ. God sent him from New Jersey, then down to Crescent City. When I was going to a psychiatrist, he encouraged me through the years. He once told me, "Mevely, you can take uppers and downers [medication] but until you accept Christ, you won't get better." And that's what I eventually did, I gave my life to Christ. I was going to make it through but there were more trials and even greater tribulations ahead.

The first of these greater tribulations was the death of my momma in 1984. I was a month pregnant, with my second daughter Devonia when she was murdered. It hit me so hard, I believe my unborn child felt the trauma. I moved into my first apartment in public housing, Rosa K. Ragsdale Apartments. It was a two-bedroom apartment. Just enough room for me, Shalonda, and eventually her baby sister Devonia. We called it home for about seven years.

My marriage was OK at first. It didn't matter what he did. He rescued me. I eventually realized because he saved me, I took a lot of mess from him. However, do not allow yourself to be abused or mistreated because you feel that you owe someone something. People wanted me to leave him, and he even said I shouldn't want anything to do with him.

However, he climbed over the walls of my broken heart, and I shared the abuse I endured. Nothing could be worse than what I had experienced as a child and a teenager. He said he'd get me some help and he did. I went to counseling traumatized, battered, wounded, and deeply scarred. I could see a tiny light at the end of my healing tunnel following each session.

I know he wasn't the best thing for me, but I know God sent him to help, so I'd know that I could make it through. God uses whom he chooses to rescue us even when it doesn't add up. He saved me again when I thought I was losing my mind. In 1988, I wanted my mom and went into a deep depression. The depression almost swallowed me whole, this was before I established a personal relationship with God. I felt hopeless. I cried hysterically.

Back then, I had to remember the prices of all the items in the store. I was at the register waiting on customers and crying.

Then I was sucker punched when I started dealing with my husband's other women harassing me. One thing was for sure, I couldn't afford to lose my mind like my momma did. I was not going to end up in a straitjacket and not be able to take care of my kids. I couldn't leave my kids with anyone and risk them being sexually abused, like me.

My mother-in-law was an excellent mom; she was a wonderful influence in my life. He'd leave me at his mom's house, and we'd stay there until he got off. His mom took care of me and her children. Even after I had surgery, she was there cleaning, cooking and providing. She was a great mother-figure, something I'd never had. Nevertheless, she accepted him for who he was [my human savior, an unfaithful husband, and her beloved son].

He got another one of his women pregnant. So, at that point, I got my tubes tied. I refused to be a baby momma or have a stepdad for my children that's why we got married. Even today, people ask me why I even talk to him. My reply is simple, "He rescued me several times, so I continue to grant him grace." We'll probably always be friends, because I am grateful for who I am with his help and God's.

I understand our lives are a translation of what "God allows" and what "God ordains." God will give us what we want and still make it purposeful. However, when something is ordained in our lives the purpose of it is pre-established versus God having to work the purpose out [so it works for our good]. We still talk. He caused a lot of hurt but he also helped me. That's why I believe, our greatest enemy can lead us to our greatest victory. Everything leads us to where we need to be, which is with Christ and in His will.

Sometimes the things we survive, others will die from. God will let us make it through, just so we can show others they, too, can make it. So baby listen, you will make it through, just hold on!

Chapter 6

The STRONG Work Behind My STRONG Faith

After my brother Freddie found momma and daddy dead, he was never the same and neither was I. In 1990, he called and asked me to come get him from Washington, DC. I boarded a Greyhound bus, and I went to see about my brother.

Later on, I found out Freddie was extremely ill. He had contracted AIDS. My husband wouldn't allow him to live with us and our three children. So, my Uncle George McRae, in Miami, helped me navigate the process of caring for someone with AIDS. Not to mention, resources were very limited during the early '90s.

Eventually, I put Freddie into a nursing home in Gainesville, Florida. In 1992, he died there… Freddie was the last living member of my immediate family. Although, people said he was gay, he didn't live that lifestyle in front of me. Freddie was my brother; I cared for him, and I didn't have any judgment for him. I loved my brother no matter what.

I've always been independent while always depending on God. Even when I didn't personally know the Lord, He knew me. That's the beauty of His grace — He knows and loves us. I worked diligently to instill my independence and hard work in my children. Because I made it through my childhood, I knew I could make it through anything. I wasn't a welfare queen, and I was not going to raise aspiring welfare queens either!

When Shalonda was a baby, I raised her for a short while on welfare, but I repaid every penny. I went to the courthouse and asked for a payment plan, and I paid installments until the balance was paid-in-full.

When Shalonda got sick at five-years-old, she had cysts in her intestines. The doctor said it was just waste, but we knew that wasn't it. Things grew worse and she ended up having surgery that resulted in a large section of her intestines being removed. We were also told she may not have children. She was a sickly child… if other kids were sick, she'd become sick too. Nevertheless, the Lord blessed her with three children. I love how God makes man out to be a liar, He always does!

Around 2011, I was headed to minister at a revival and Shalonda, and I passed each other on the road. I was coming from work and

Shalonda was headed to the mall. When I drove past her, the Lord said, "Don't skip a beat". I thought that was God preparing me for the revival. I ran home and jumped in the shower. Then there was a knock on the door. I could hear a voice faintly. When I opened the door Shalonda was on the ground. I was wrapped in a bath towel and helped her into the house. I made sure Shalonda was OK, and I went on to complete the assignment at church.

Things got worse with Shalonda's health, and she still tried to work. We purchased a home and moved in together. As a concerned mom, I didn't want to leave her home alone. God spoke two words: Trust Me. My job started implementing changes. They moved me to the grocery store in Crescent City. God sent four angels that would look after Shalonda when I had to work. Sherry Walker, Diane Williams [she is my soul friend and consistent prayer partner], Kim Spell, and Shalonda's best friend, Tamara Thomas.

As the days went by, I listened to a song that said *you have to trust me when you can't trace me.* I would leave for work and would close my eyes. Shalonda went from a size 14 to a size four. Unfortunately, I knew I couldn't quit my job.

I saw a billboard advertising insurance that I passed every single day but this particular day, my eyes locked to it. It read, "A promise made, is a promise kept". At that moment, I knew she would be OK. We went to the doctor who said, "You're living with a dead woman, but I'll do what I can to get her back to health." At that point, it was the two of us. This is the child I know God gave me to rescue me and it was my time to repay the favor. It was my reasonable service.

When Shalonda was sick, she didn't drive and couldn't take care of her children like she desired. After numerous visits to the doctor, we finally went to Mayo Clinic and Shalonda was diagnosed with fibromyalgia, chronic fatigue syndrome, and Hashimoto Thyroiditis. She didn't leave the house unless it was a doctor's appointment. There were days when my faith dwindled. I was her caretaker. One day my nerves were at the bottom. We both were having a bad day and I shook her. I couldn't believe I got to that point, but we never talked about it again.

I received a call from a lady in Orlando named Martha Newman. She and her husband Alan traveled from Orlando to Palatka weekly to encourage Shalonda's spirit and have bible study with her. Martha told me, "It's time for Shalonda to get up." They called and encouraged Shalonda, and she got up. To this day, she considers Martha as her spiritual mother.

Then one day, Shalonda asked for my car keys, and by faith, I placed the keys in her hands.

About five years after Shalonda's recovery, my daughter Neshia also became deathly ill. She was in the hospital and septic. Shalonda called and informed me that things weren't looking good. I spoke to God after I hung up the phone and said, "OK, God, don't take this child from me." I don't know whose faith kicked in faster, mine or Shalonda's but Neisha walked out of the hospital fully recovered. Doctors later found out that she was severely anemic. Again, God reminded me that I would make it through it [and so would my children and my children's children]! God has been so good to us!

Looking back over my life, I didn't think I'd live to be 25 not to mention 50. God's grace brings me to tears of joy! He turned every unfavorable situation in my life around — in my favor! The hurt, the betrayals, the abuse, or anything that has wounded me has not made me bitter, unforgiving, or unloving. In fact, it has done the exact opposite. I am grateful to God because I did not become what was done to me by others, but I became who God has been to me. God loves me, so I love others. God gives me grace, so I give others grace. God gives me LIFE, so I plant seeds that will guarantee a harvest that proves God is my everything. Therefore, everything I do *must* please Him. It is my reasonable service unto God... all to Thee I owe.

Nevertheless, Shalonda decorated my 50th birthday celebration [that God allowed me to see], and it was beautiful. From this event, she birthed Bad Hands Event Planning & Decor. God gave her a gift and she's been a very successful entrepreneur. So, the promise made was, indeed, the promise God kept. He's allowed my daughter to *still* be here, and she is making it through.

Two house fires

I've been involved in two house fires and God brought me through both. In 2015, when I arrived at the first fire, there were firefighters everywhere. I was told, "Don't go inside". The kitchen and attic were fully consumed. I was able to save about 20 percent of my personal items but due to smoke and water damage, I almost lost everything. And when it seemed matters couldn't get any worse, a legal battle happened because it was a rental home. But God worked that out, too.

A couple years later, God allowed me to recover all, and I paid cash for the next house. My new home was beautiful, it was everything I desired! Unfortunately, in 2017, it also caught fire while I was out of town on a girl's trip. This fire happened on a Friday. It ravaged everything in its path, leaving with me with two skirts and the clothes in my suitcase from the trip. My kids didn't tell me the extent of the damage. Nevertheless, this repeated misfortune was the result of a grease fire. Thankfully, no one was injured, but the house had to be gutted and completely renovated. However, this, too, was a blessing!

This particular year presented quite a few tribulations. Devonia was pregnant and I was very excited about being a grandma *again*. This baby was going to complete our family because she was the only one who didn't have any children.

That Monday following the fire, Shalonda called, and I could tell by the sound of her voice, it wasn't good news. She said, "The baby is gone, and I don't know if they'll be able to save Vonia." Within 48 hours, the house was gone, and my daughter's life was on the line. On the drive back to Florida, we got pulled over twice in two different states. My daughter called again, and said, "I don't think she'll make it." So, I called my pastor with a strong prayerful demand. I said, "Listen, my baby better be in Palatka when I get there." He said, "OK...she will be here." With tears streaming down my face, my friend Faye drove and uttered a simple prayer, "Lord, please save my daughter's life." God was faithful to me *again*. He brought us through it! I know I am not exempt from the possibility of losing a child, I'm just grateful that I haven't. The Lord is gracious and so kind!

Chapter 7

My Shining Starr

When I first found out Shalonda was pregnant, I was mad, although she was 19 and grown. Nevertheless, we want our children to be 1,000 times better than us. My mom used to call Shalonda her little star. Therefore, Shalonda knew she would name her first daughter Shastarra.

When I warmed up to the idea that I would be a grandmother, I got excited. Most parents decorate a nursery for the baby, but I redesigned my whole house. I did my own bedroom over. I had new carpet, paint and furniture because I knew she was going to be a special child. As a little girl, she was quiet, humble, and sometimes moody. She took care of everyone, but would sometimes bully her younger sister. Starra helped take care of her siblings. At 16, Starra got a car because she proved to be responsible. On her bad days, she warned me by saying, "Go on grandma, I'm having a bad day." Not even adults give this warning, some just take their frustrations out on you. Everybody loves Starra. Even her godparents have always been a strong support to her throughout her life.

When she was losing her eyesight in her junior year of high school, I attended her doctor visits in faith believing God would do it. Although I pushed through, I had no choice because I had to be strong for her as well as her mom, Shalonda.

I remember going to church when a local pastor spoke to me and said, "It *will* work." I thought he was talking about Starra's sight being restored, and it was. While it didn't work out the way we thought it would, it *still* worked. She was losing sight in her left eye and the doctors prevented her vision from deteriorating in her right eye. It worked! She isn't legally blind and can still see [glory be to God]!

Starra has the strength of a giant [to me]. She's well rounded and this gives me joy. Starra is the strength for everybody and cares for everyone. I guess she gets it from her grandmother. It's just in us to love people like God loves us...without conditions. While I haven't always loved like Christ, I must admit that loving like God is an inside job.

Then there's my other granddaughter Meliyah, who wasn't supposed to be here. Shalonda was told to abort her at seven months because she was missing the stem at the top of her spine. The doctor was convinced that

Meliyah would be a vegetable (and completely paralyzed for life). I told Shalonda to wait and we're going to trust God. I talked to God, and He said, "No". When Meliyah was born, she was completely healthy... she made it through it!

I remember when I first got saved, Mother Youman helped me with some amazing words of wisdom, she said, "Can't 'cha take wrong and go 'head? Because as long as you're right with God, you don't have anything to prove." Eventually, I got it. I've learned to please God and everything else will fall into place. Not only have I learned to make it through, I also learned to love and forgive, sincerely. These are key to making it through.

I don't take the abundance I have experienced in my life for granted. I can recall sitting at the city dock and looking around one day. The Lord spoke, "Look at the bridge, look at the clock, and look at the cars. That stuff is all man made. Now look at water, sky, and birds...Nobody can take credit for those things except Me." My response was simple, "And no one can take credit for my life but God."

Chapter 8

Church Drama & Trauma — You Can Make It Through That, Too
~God

I've been in the church most of my life. In fact, I gave my life to Christ in 1987. I knew then that I desperately needed something real… a sustainable and everlasting hope. I needed the keeper and the comforter, the lion and the lamb, and the Holy Spirit. I have always had a love for serving people [believers and unbelievers, alike] because we're all God's children. Some of us just don't know it or haven't received Him yet. I must admit, I'm guilty of overextending myself while serving people, especially those in leadership positions in the church. I've taken classes on serving in leadership so that I could serve pastors well. Thankfully, I have learned we should never blur the fine lines of serving or esteeming people more than we serve and esteem God-that's dangerous. There's a difference between having a need and being needed; however, I know what it's like to need someone and no one's there. This is why I live and serve the way I do.

Nevertheless, God has called each of us to a special role in the body of Christ. My calling is to live a life that will lead others to Him [no tricks, no gimmicks, and no religious rules]. I want people to know that God is *real*. And I deeply desire to lead others to Christ by showing love because I know God loves us, unconditionally! The word of God declares that the world will know us by the love we have for one another. Therefore, our love and compassion must be clearly identifiable from afar and up close.

I was given the title of evangelist years ago, but before the title, I already had a special gift of compassion and love for people. When we are called to serve in ministry (in any capacity), we see all sides of people, including the sides we don't want to see or deal with. This is why prayer must be our first resort, daily. It is our responsibility to see the good in others as well as help them to see the good in themselves. God put something good inside every one of us as He fashioned us in our mother's womb (in His image).

I earnestly believe the very things the enemy attempted to strip away from me [love, compassion, and forgiveness], are the very things that cause my cup to run over, today. Therefore, I will not allow my title as an evangelist to supersede God's assignment or plans for my life. Titles are given by man to maintain systems that will not influence where any of us will spend eternity. In fact, I believe when *too much* "weight" is placed on a title/position, it causes haughtiness, contention, envy, and strife in the body of Christ. Particularly, when there's a hunger for power versus a hunger to love like Christ and accept *all* people right where they are. I had to learn; titles don't move God. And when I understood this, I realized God was moved by my obedience to Him. So do not allow those with titles to supersede what God tells you to do. This is why I believe that sometimes it's better to be a "pew saint" than an exalted leader because when leaders fall, people fall with them. This explains why our trust should always be in God and *not* man.

Additionally, titles in any capacity, have a natural tendency to make a person feel proud and that's OK. We should be proud to serve in ministry and in our communities. However, the cornerstones of faith [love, patience, humility and forgiveness] should keep us as humble servants. Furthermore, titles lead far too many of us to behave as judges and not servants. Therefore, we cannot allow the attention that titles potentially bring cause us to forget why we gave our lives to Christ, in the first place.

One of the first lessons God presented to me was in forgiveness. I had to forgive a murderer, molester and a rapist (my stepfather). Surely, if I could learn to love through that kind of pain, trauma, and dysfunction, I could love church folks who are oftentimes messy and jacked up! Honestly, there's no comparison. However, for some reason believers believe the church, the pastor and members are perfect. Well, that's a lie from

Hell! I have been saved for more than 30 years and I still have to ask God to save me from myself [almost daily]. Eventually, we discover those in the faith say and do hurtful things because they attempt to follow religious rules, instead of following Godly principles for righteous living.

Nevertheless, I must credit believers for maturing me. These individuals taught me that I would make it through whatever I was going through, even if they were the blame. There have been times when I almost threw in the towel (on the church), but definitely not God. However, I just couldn't bring myself to do it because I didn't want to diminish my testimony and more importantly, bring any shame to God's name; He has been too good to me! Instead, when uncomfortable situations arise, the Lord softens my heart and gives me a right spirit to handle the matter without being bitter. Now I have to confess that I have been angry (countless times). However, I've learned to give God's people the same thing we give our mean bosses, rude mother-in-laws, nasty next-door neighbors, mean stepparents, and disobedient children-grace! As true believers, we don't get to say, "I don't fool with him, her or them." What if God blessed us and then decided He would not fool with us? Oh, what a tragedy it would be! Now I am not saying allow someone to misuse you. I am saying, speak in love, set boundaries, release, and bless them. God's mercies are new every morning and we desperately need them (all of us)! So, we must grow to a place of loving like Him, but first we have to ask Him to do just that.

I remember when a position I held was eliminated throughout the company. Although

I was offered other positions, I was upset! I wanted to quit, but I didn't... just like I didn't quit fellowshipping at church when things got hard. Life is a series of tests, particularly for believers. We must understand that we will be tested in every area of our lives. This includes in our home, in our place of work, in our finances, through family members and of course in the church, especially if we attend regularly. James 1:2-4 NIV tells of the trials we will face in life and to persevere through them. These passages of scripture also remind us that the only way to make it through is to keep our eyes on Jesus.

Consider it pure joy, my brothers and sisters, whenever you face trials of many kinds, because you know that the testing of your faith produces perseverance. Let perseverance finish its work so that you may be mature and complete, not lacking anything.

Additionally, Job 14:1 states that our days are full of trouble. *Man, that is born of a woman is of few days, and full of trouble.*

Psalm 27:5 reminds us that in the time of trouble, God will hide us. It reads: *For in the time of trouble He shall hide me in His pavilion; In the secret place of His tabernacle, He shall hide me; He shall set me high upon a rock.*

This scripture doesn't say we should run and hide. Therefore, we will experience challenging situations and downright difficult people. Their purpose is to grow and stretch us (even though they may stress us). We can't eat applesauce all of our saved lives and never experience solid foods! Not only will we go through things but *grow* through them. We must accept the fact that people (saved and unsaved) are flawed and nowhere near perfect.

If that was the case, there would be no need for Christ's finished work on the cross.

Do not allow your relationship with your pastor to supersede your relationship with God. In fact, no relationship should take the place of one who created us and gave His life for us. Respect your leaders, receive their guidance, and listen to God. When we stand before God no one (and I mean no one), will be able to answer for us.

So, my best advice to those dealing with church hurt or trauma is to pray for your pastor in the same manner you did when you first joined the church. Don't you dare create a clique or pick up the phone to discuss the decisions that you don't agree with or his transgressions or anyone else's. Pastors are imperfect people serving a perfect God (we all are). Instead, ask God to grow you in this area of your life. Our job as believers is to be quick to listen (examine the information) and be slow to speak (remain fervent in prayer). If you don't have peace about a situation, go back and pray again. Lastly, ask God for direction and wait to hear His instructions...this means to wait in prayer. When God gives you the response/plan, follow it closely and of course, do all things in love, even if it's time to move on. Have a conversation, avoid gossip and be discreet as possible in your departure. The world is watching us. Remember, we are all human beings in need of God's new mercies daily.

Now pastors and leaders, you are the watchers and caretakers of your members. You should never take advantage of anyone or abuse your power (in the name of God); thereby, causing harm to members. If God called you, then remember just that: God called you to serve by feeding His sheep, not beating them! Serving as a leader comes with great responsibility. The word that you preach to the congregation, must be the words that convict you to righteousness living, first. We will be held accountable for our words and deeds, known and unknown, intentional, and unintentional.

Sin is the great separator that can cause any of us, leaders included, to end up in situations that results in a heavy price to pay, in this life and in the life to come, if we don't repent.

When I find myself in uncertain situations, I always ask God to fix me, and He fixes the situation. This is the importance of meditating on and applying God's word to our lives. The more we commune with God, the more we take on His character, particularly in the body of Christ and especially in the church (from the ushers to the pulpit).

So, pastors and leaders, serve the people well but take care of yourself, too. And when you find yourself not being your best self, ask your congregation to pray with you. Now, I leave you with the same words (from on high) that have encouraged me throughout my life. No matter what you face... You can make it through. ~God

My favorite scripture, Isaiah 43:2 states, "When you pass through the waters, I will be with you; and when you pass through the rivers, they will not sweep over you. When you walk through the fire, you will not be burned; the flames will not set you ablaze."

Homage to Our Mother

Ma, you epitomize the beauty of God's love, which is selfless, reliant, and irreplaceable. You are our pillar. We can depend on YOU for everything. Ma, you've been the constant presence in our lives that proves God is real! Additionally, we understand that the unconditional love we experience comes from God's people and, we know that you are God's people! However, we are eternally grateful that you're our mother.

We appreciate your natural ability to LISTEN wholeheartedly without judgment… This is love in action and it shows that YOU truly care! Ma, you provide counsel to those who seek advice and your "wise-real-life" approach to loving others is divine. You are the most caring, accepting, and humorously straightforward woman we love and know.

Consequently, we understand why so many people are drawn to YOU. Ma, your aura says, "Let me love on you." Does it annoy us a little? Yes. So, we will tell the truth, and shame the devil! However, as God-lovers and your daughters, we recognize that your life is the miraculous proof that people can make it through anything, *with* God! Therefore, we are grateful that the love YOU give is so genuine that YOUR presence can't be denied.

The stretch of YOUR love is as deep as God's love for YOU — it is gracious and merciful. For this reason, we willingly share YOU with the world. We are eternally grateful that you shower us with your love *daily* because we wouldn't be who we are *without* YOU!

We are extremely proud of you, and BLESSED to have you as our Ma!

We love you eternally,

Shalonda M. Spell

Devonia L. Spell

Darneshia L. Spell

About the Author

Mevely Spell is so much more than what meets the eye. The impact her life has made on others is miraculous! This Florida native is a mother, entrepreneur, evangelist, and now a published author! Her debut literary work, "Listen… You Can Make It Through This. ~ God," is a riveting account of what happens when and if we TRUST God with every facet of our lives.

Ms. Mevely's life is a beacon of hope that proves God never breaks a promise. Everything that happens to us, is an opportunity for God to show UP for us! Mevely can attest to this fact, when God is with us, everything that happens to us works out for the best… And nothing compares to this blessed assurance. Therefore, Mevely stands firmly on God's word.

In her downtime, Mevely loves spending time with her family and friends, laughing until her side hurts, and having intimate conversations with God. For more information about Mevely Spell, please visit www.motivatedbymevely.com.